ANIMAL FAMILIES

The Hawk Family

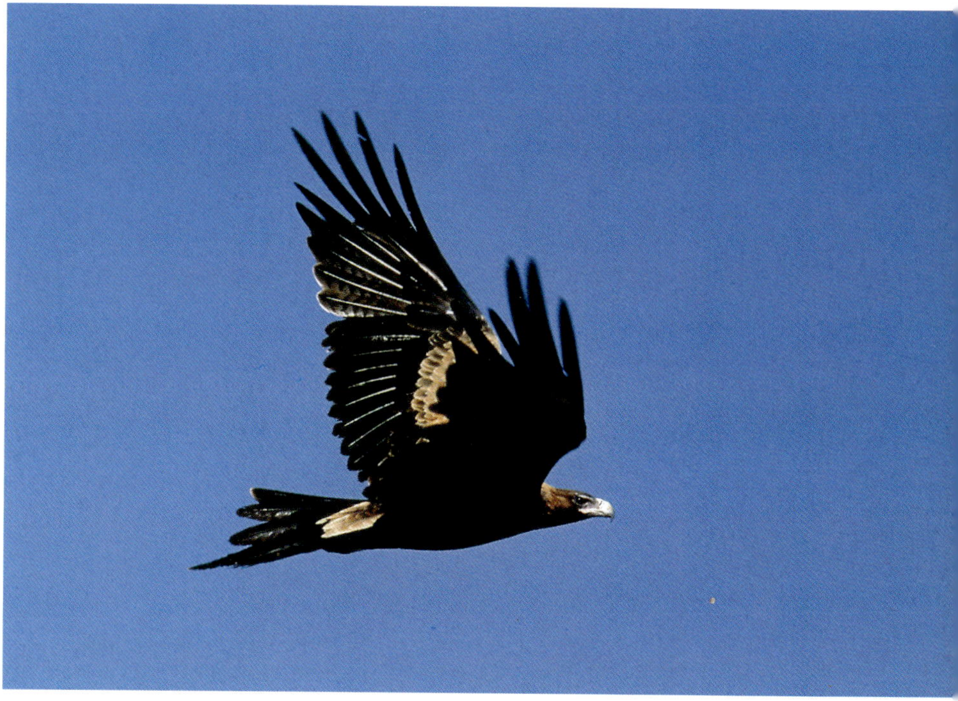

Bev Harvey

This edition first published in 2004 in the United States of America by Chelsea Clubhouse, a division of Chelsea House Publishers and a subsidiary of Haights Cross Communications.

All rights reserved. No part of this publication may be reproduced or transmitted in any form or by any means without the written permission of the publisher.

Chelsea Clubhouse
1974 Sproul Road, Suite 400
Broomall, PA 19008-0914

The Chelsea House world wide web address is www.chelseahouse.com

Library of Congress Cataloging-in-Publication Data

Harvey, Bev.
   The hawk family / Bev Harvey.
   p. cm. — (Animal families)
   Summary: Simple text compares and contrasts members of the hawk family in terms of where they live, body features, eating habits, and size. Species featured include the northern goshawk, Cooper's hawk, golden eagle, wedge-tailed eagle, bald eagle, white-bellied sea eagle, whistling kite, and northern harrier.
   ISBN 0-7910-7544-3
   1. Accipitridae—Juvenile literature. [1. Hawk family (Birds)] I. Title. II. Series.
   QL696.F32H375 2004
   598.9'4—dc21

2002155661

First published in 2003 by
MACMILLAN EDUCATION AUSTRALIA PTY LTD
627 Chapel Street, South Yarra, Australia, 3141

Associated companies and representatives throughout the world.

Copyright © Bev Harvey 2003
Copyright in photographs © individual photographers as credited

Edited by Angelique Campbell-Muir
Page layout by Domenic Lauricella
Photo research by Sarah Saunders

Printed in China

Acknowledgements
The author and the publisher are grateful to the following for permission to reproduce copyright material:

Cover photograph: wedge-tailed eagle in flight, courtesy of ANT Photo Library.

ANT Photo Library, pp. 1, 5, 7 (top), 21; John Cancalosi/Auscape, pp. 6 (center), 16; Peter Cook/Auscape, p. 4 (top); Jean-Paul Ferrero/Auscape, p. 26; Jeff Foott/Auscape, pp. 6 (top), 15; John Shaw/Auscape, pp. 7 (bottom), 28; Lynn M. Stone/Auscape, pp. 7 (center), 22; Australian Picture Library/Corbis, pp. 17, 19; Coo-ee Picture Library, pp. 8–9, 20, 25; Getty Images, pp. 6 (bottom), 10, 11, 18, 23; Jiri Lochman/Lochman Transparencies, pp. 4 (bottom), 24, 27; Photolibrary.com, pp. 14, 29.

While every care has been taken to trace and acknowledge copyright, the publisher tenders their apologies for any accidental infringement where copyright has proved untraceable. Where the attempt has been unsuccessful, the publisher welcomes information that would redress the situation.

Contents

Animal Families	4
Where Hawks Live	6
Hawk Features	8
Hawks as Hunters	10
The Size of Hawks	12
Hawks	14
Eagles	18
Whistling Kites	26
Northern Harriers	28
Common and Scientific Names	30
Glossary	31
Index	32

Animal Families

Scientists group similar kinds of animals together. They call these groups families. The animals that belong to each family share similar features.

The hawk family

Hawks, eagles, kites, and harriers all belong to the hawk family. They build nests in trees, on cliffs, or on the ground. They live where they can find **prey** to hunt.

Bald eagles build giant nests in trees.

Where Hawks Live

Northern goshawks are found in mountain and forest areas of North America, Europe, and Asia.

Cooper's hawks live in southern Canada and the northern United States, but they travel as far south as Central America during winter.

Golden eagles are found in parts of Europe, Asia, northern Africa, and North America.

Wedge-tailed eagles are found in Australia and New Guinea.

Bald eagles' range covers most of North America, from Alaska and northern Canada to the southwestern United States.

Northern harriers spend summers in Alaska, Canada, and the northern United States. In winter, they are found in the southern United States and Central America.

Hawk Features

Members of the hawk family have many features in common.

feathers for flying

long tail for steering

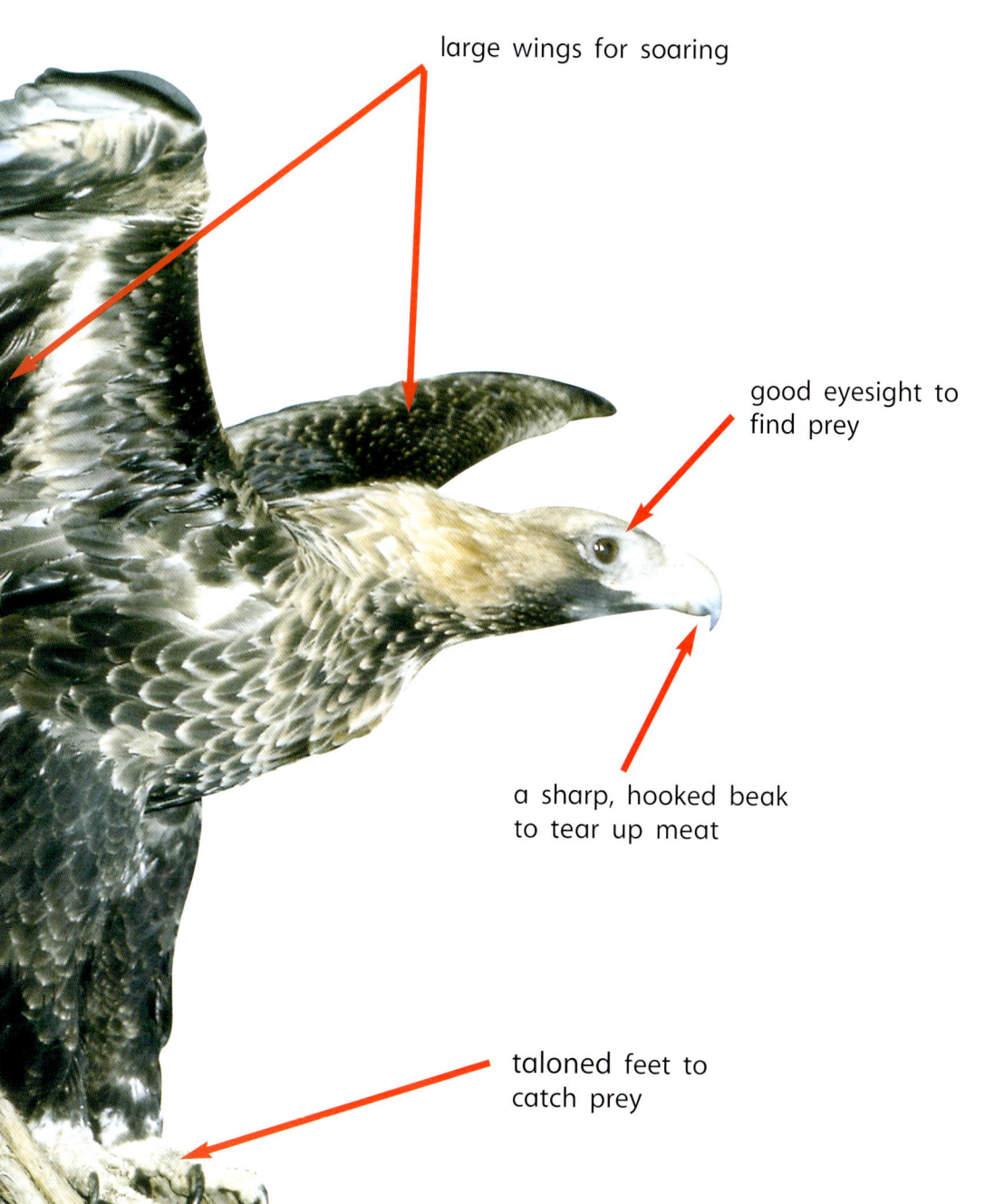

Hawks as Hunters

Birds in the hawk family are called birds of prey. They are good hunters. They have good eyesight and watch for prey to catch.

Some hawk family members watch for prey while soaring through the air.

Birds in the hawk family have strong talons to catch and squeeze prey.

Members of the hawk family are **carnivores**. They hunt rabbits, fish, birds, and snakes. They hunt during the day. They grip their prey so tightly that they squeeze them to death.

The Size of Hawks

Hawk family members are different sizes. Eagles have large wings for soaring. Hawks that live in forests, like the goshawk, have small wings for flying among the trees.

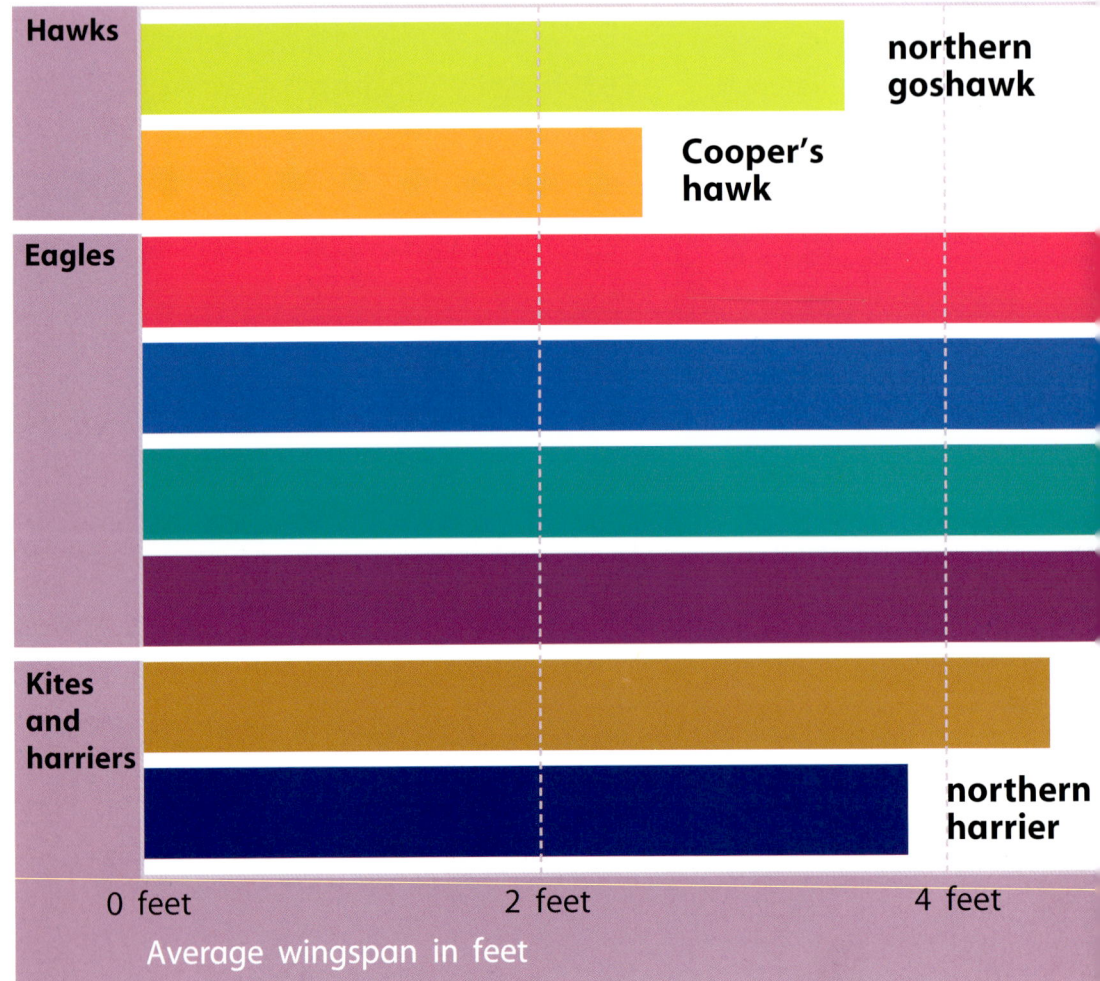

Average wingspan in feet

Birds are measured by their **wingspan**.

golden eagle

wedge-tailed eagle

bald eagle

white-bellied sea eagle

whistling kite

6 feet   8 feet

Hawks

Hawks have short, strong wings to help them take off swiftly. They use their long tail as a **rudder** to dart and dive quickly. Hawks can catch their prey while flying in the air, or when landing on the ground.

Hawks usually spot their prey while perched on a branch. Then they take flight.

Northern goshawks

Northern goshawks live in forests. They can quickly dart in and out of trees and under branches. A pair of goshawks may build a few nests in the range where they live. They mostly use one nest at a time.

Northern goshawks typically have two to three chicks.

Cooper's hawks

The Cooper's hawk is also called a chicken hawk because it sometimes catches chickens. The Cooper's hawk also hunts squirrels and chipmunks.

The Cooper's hawk has a sharply hooked bill.

A Cooper's hawk waits on its perch until its prey looks away, then it takes flight.

A Cooper's hawk will sit on a **perch** watching for prey. Then it will swoop down and catch it. Sometimes it will chase its prey while half flying and half running along the ground.

Eagles

Eagles are like hawks except they are larger. They have a wide wingspan and very good eyesight. Eagles are powerful birds of prey.

The golden eagle is the largest bird of prey in North America.

Golden eagles

A golden eagle will stay with the same **mate** for life. When golden eagles hunt together one eagle will chase the prey. Once the prey is tired from being chased, the other eagle swoops down and catches it.

A golden eagle hunts with its mate.

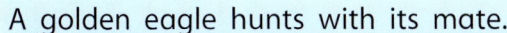

Wedge-tailed eagles

The wedge-tailed eagle is a big, strong hunter. It hunts rabbits and small kangaroos.

Wedge-tailed eagles' legs have feathers all the way down to the talons.

Wedge-tailed eagles can fly at heights of up to 6,500 feet (2,000 meters).

People used to hunt and kill wedge-tailed eagles until there were not many left living in the wild. Now the eagles are protected from hunters.

Bald eagles

The bald eagle lives near water. If its water supply freezes, it will fly to warmer weather.

Bald eagles eat mostly fish, so they need to live near water.

While watching for prey, bald eagles soar on air currents.

Bald eagles often soar high on **thermals**, or columns, of warm air. They glide down until they find another thermal to take them up again.

White-bellied sea eagles

The white-bellied sea eagle builds its nest in a tall tree or on a rock high up on a cliff by the water. It has high perches so it can look out for prey.

A white-bellied sea eagle uses the same nest each year.

The white-bellied sea eagle is mostly found along the coast and near large rivers and lakes in Australia.

The white-bellied sea eagle likes to eat sea snakes. It waits for sea snakes to come up to the water's surface to breathe. Then it skims across the water and grabs the snake with its talons.

Whistling Kites

The whistling kite has a loud call that sounds like a whistle. It calls throughout the day and at dusk.

The whistling kite is common in Australia.

Whistling kites are often found near water.

The whistling kite hunts mainly rabbits. It also eats small animals, lizards, fish, and insects. The whistling kite eats carrion, or dead animals, as well.

Northern Harriers

The face of the northern harrier looks like an owl's face. The feathers on the northern harrier's face point sound to its ears so it can hear its prey when it is hunting.

Northern harriers' eyes turn from brown to gold as they become adults.

Northern harriers usually hunt mice, but they also eat insects and small reptiles.

The male northern harrier dives, twirls, and spins in the air to attract a mate. The female lays her eggs in a nest on the ground.

Common and Scientific Names

The scientific name for the hawk family is Accipitridae. There are about 220 types of birds in the hawk family. These are the common and scientific names of the ones in this book:

Accipitridae family		
Common name	**Scientific names:**	
	Genus	**Species**
northern goshawk	*Accipiter*	*gentilis*
Cooper's hawk	*Accipiter*	*cooperii*
golden eagle	*Aquila*	*chrysaetos*
wedge-tailed eagle	*Aquila*	*audax*
bald eagle	*Haliaeetus*	*leucocephalus*
white-bellied sea eagle	*Haliaeetus*	*leucogaster*
whistling kite	*Haliastur*	*sphenurus*
northern harrier	*Circus*	*cyaneus*

Glossary

carnivores	meat-eating animals
genus	the name for a large group of similar animals within an animal family; the genus is the first part of the scientific name of an animal
mate	one of a male and female pair
perch	a place where a bird can sit and rest
prey	an animal that is hunted for food
rudder	something that is used for steering
species	a group of animals that are closely related and can produce young; the species is the second part of the scientific name of an animal
talons	the claws of a bird that can grab prey
thermals	rising currents of warm air
wingspan	the distance between the tips of a bird's wings

Index

b
beak 4, 9

c
carnivore 11

e
eggs 29
eyesight 4, 9, 10

f
feathers 8, 28
flying 8, 12, 14, 17, 22, 23, 29
food 9, 11, 16, 17, 19, 20, 25, 27

m
mate 19, 29

n
nest 5, 15, 24, 29

p
perch 17, 24
prey 5, 9, 10, 11, 14, 17, 18, 19, 20, 24, 25, 27, 28

r
rabbits 11, 27

s
size 12–13
soaring 9, 10, 12, 23

t
talons 4, 9, 25
thermal 23

w
water 22, 24, 25
wings 4, 9, 12, 14, 18
wingspan 12–13, 18